KATIE LEDECKY

OLYMPIC SWIMMER

KATIE LAJINESS

Big Buddy Books

An Imprint of Abdo Publishing
abdopublishing.com

BIG BUDDY OLYMPIC BIOGRAPHIES

abdopublishing.com

Published by Abdo Publishing, a division of ABDO, PO Box 398166, Minneapolis, Minnesota 55439.
Copyright © 2017 by Abdo Consulting Group, Inc. International copyrights reserved in all countries.
No part of this book may be reproduced in any form without written permission from the publisher.
Big Buddy Books™ is a trademark and logo of Abdo Publishing.

Printed in the United States of America, North Mankato, Minnesota.
102016
012017

THIS BOOK CONTAINS
RECYCLED MATERIALS

Cover Photo: epa european pressphoto agency b.v./Alamy Stock Photo
Interior Photos: Aflo Co. Ltd./Alamy Stock Photo (p. 29); ASSOCIATED PRESS (pp. 9, 11, 15, 17, 21, 23, 25, 27); Chris Schmid Photography/Alamy Stock Photo (p. 19); epa european pressphoto agency b.v./Alamy Stock Photo (p. 29); © IStockphoto.com (p. 29); Joe Scarnici/Stringer (p. 13); REUTERS/Alamy Stock Photo (p. 5); Xinhua/Alamy Stock Photo (p. 31).

Coordinating Series Editor: Tamara L. Britton
Graphic Design: Jenny Christensen

Publisher's Cataloging-in-Publication Data

Names: Lajiness, Katie, author.
Title: Katie Ledecky / by Katie Lajiness.
Description: Minneapolis, MN : Abdo Publishing, 2017. | Series: Big buddy Olympic biographies | Includes bibliographical references and index.
Identifiers: LCCN 2016953148 | ISBN 9781680785531 (lib. bdg.) | ISBN 9781680785814 (ebook)
Subjects: LCSH: Ledecky, Katie, 1997- --Juvenile literature. | Swimmers--United States--Biography--Juvenile literature. | Women Olympic athletes--United States--Biography--Juvenile literature. | Olympic Games (31st : 2016 : Rio de Janeiro, Brazil)
Classification: DDC 797.2/1092 [B]--dc23
LC record available at http://lccn.loc.gov/2016953148

CONTENTS

SWIMMING CHAMPION

Katie Ledecky is one of the fastest swimmers in the world. She has won **medals** at the Olympics, the FINA World **Championships**, and the Pan Pacific Championships. Many believe Katie is one of the greatest female swimmers of all time.

SNAPSHOT

NAME: Kathleen "Katie" Genevieve Ledecky

BIRTHDAY: March 17, 1997

BIRTHPLACE: Washington, DC

TURNED PROFESSIONAL: Amateur

OLYMPIC MEDALS WON: 5 gold, 1 silver

CHAMPIONSHIPS: FINA World Championships and Pan Pacific

FAMILY TIES

Katie was born in Washington, DC, on March 17, 1997. Her full name is Kathleen Genevieve Ledecky.

Katie's parents are David and Mary Genevieve Ledecky. Her older brother is Michael. Katie's family lives in Bethesda, Maryland.

WHERE IN THE WORLD?

Pennsylvania

Ohio

Maryland

New Jersey

Delaware

West Virginia

Washington
DC

Kentucky

Virginia

ATLANTIC
OCEAN

Tennessee

North Carolina

N
W E
S

EARLY YEARS

Katie started swimming at age six after her brother joined a swim team. Katie was a natural talent! She was soon swimming in **competitions**.

DID YOU KNOW ?

Katie's brother was on the swim team at Harvard University. Her mother swam for the University of New Mexico.

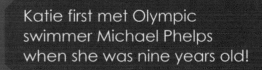

Katie first met Olympic swimmer Michael Phelps when she was nine years old!

STARTING OUT

When Katie was ten, she began training with **coach** Yuri Suguiyama. She trained at the Nation's Capital Swim Club. By age 14, Katie was already setting national records.

Katie proved to be a tough **competitor**. In 2011, she won the 400-, 800-, and 1500-meter freestyle at the US Junior **Championships**.

Coach Yuri taught Katie to swim like Michael Phelps. She copied his stroke and kicked her legs hard to swim faster.

Many changes were in store for Katie. When Katie was 15, her **coach** moved to California. So, she began working with a new coach.

Bruce Gemmell helped Katie improve her athletic ability. He had her do exercises outside the pool, too. Soon Katie became stronger and swam faster.

Katie does what her coach tells her so she can be the best swimmer. Coach Gemmell says she is as tough as nails.

BIG DREAMS

   As a teenager, Katie was already one of the nation's most talented swimmers. And, she kept dreaming big. After winning national **competitions**, she aimed for the Olympics. Despite a busy school schedule, Katie continued to train for the Olympic **trials**.

Katie poses for photos with her fans. Many young swimmers look up to her.

LONDON OLYMPICS

At the US Olympic **trials** in 2012, Katie swam the 800-meter freestyle. She led from the start and finished with a record time of 8:19.78 minutes. This earned her a spot on the Olympic swim team!

DID YOU KNOW ?

Katie is 6 feet (1.8 m) tall. Many female Olympic swimmers are taller than Katie.

At 15 years old, Katie was the youngest member of the 2012 US Olympic swim team.

Katie traveled to London, England, to **compete** in the games. There, she set another record in the 800-meter freestyle. Katie earned her first Olympic gold **medal**!

At the 2012 Olympics, Katie swam the 800-meter freestyle in 8:14.63 minutes. This was more than four seconds faster than the second-place winner.

A NEW GOAL

Katie had a new **goal** when she returned home from the London Olympics. She wanted to be in the 2016 Olympics! Katie continued to train hard. She was often in the pool at 5:00 a.m. Sometimes, Katie swam as much as 30 hours per week.

In 2015, Katie set a world record in the 800-meter freestyle at the FINA World Championships in Kazan, Russia.

In 2013, Katie won the FINA Best Female Swimmer award.

RIO OLYMPICS

Katie easily earned a spot on the 2016 US Olympic swim team. Again, she was the youngest member of the team.

In Rio de Janeiro, Brazil, Katie **competed** in two team and three individual events. Swimming in many different races is hard. But she stayed calm.

Katie (*left*) won the 400-meter freestyle by nearly five seconds!

Katie's first event was the 4x100-meter freestyle relay. She and her three teammates set a new American record. They won a silver **medal**.

Next, Katie swam the 400-meter freestyle. She won a gold medal and set a new world record. Katie also struck gold in the 200-meter freestyle and the 4x200-meter freestyle relay.

In her last event, Katie smashed another world record in the 800-meter freestyle. She won the gold medal.

Katie's 4x200-meter relay team beat second-place Australia by 1.84 seconds!

Katie is the first swimmer since 1968 to win the 200-, 400-, and 800-meter freestyle at the same Olympics.

OUT OF THE WATER

Katie is one of the most famous swimmers in the world. When she's not in the pool, she also volunteers with many **charities**.

As a star **athlete**, Katie is popular with the media. She has appeared on the cover of *Swimming World* magazine. Katie also appeared on the TV show *TODAY*.

In 2016, Katie threw the first pitch before a Washington Nationals baseball game.

BUZZ

In the fall of 2016, Katie entered Stanford University in Stanford, California. She joined the school's swim team.

Katie hopes to swim in the 2020 Olympics in Tokyo, Japan. Fans are excited to see what's next for Katie Ledecky!

The women's swim team at Stanford University is number two in the country.

Olympic champion swimmers Maya DiRado (top) and Simone Manuel (bottom) also swam for Stanford University.

GLOSSARY

athlete a person who is trained or skilled in sports.

championship a game, a match, or a race held to find a first-place winner.

charity a group or a fund that helps people in need.

coach someone who teaches or trains a person or a group on a certain subject or skill.

competition (kahm-puh-TIH-shuhn) a contest between two or more persons or groups. To compete is to take part in a competition. A competitor is a person who competes.

goal something that a person works to reach or complete.

medal an award for success.

trial a test of someone's ability to do something that is used to see if he or she should join a team, perform in a play, etc.

WEBSITES

To learn more about Olympic Biographies, visit **booklinks.abdopublishing.com**.
These links are routinely monitored and updated to provide
the most current information available.

INDEX